AF291395

BIG PICTURE PRESS

First published in the UK in 2026 by Big Picture Press,
an imprint of Bonnier Books UK
5th Floor, HYLO, 105 Bunhill Row,
London, EC1Y 8LZ
The authorised representative in the EEA
is Bonnier Books UK (Ireland) Limited.
Registered office address:
Block B, The Crescent Building
Northwood, Santry
Dublin 9, D09 C6X8, Ireland
compliance@bonnierbooks.ie
www.bonnierbooks.co.uk

1 3 5 7 9 10 8 6 4 2

ISBN 978-1-80078-710-0

This book was typeset in Jungle Giant and Stupid Questions
The illustrations were created digitally

Edited by Charlie Wilson
Designed by Sarah Crookes
Production by Giulia Caparrelli

Printed in China

On the Streets of
New York
A poetic tour of the city

Sarah Kay

Ryan Johnson

BPP

Poems and Postcards from New York City

When I write poems, I always feel like I am sending a postcard from the current moment I am in to whoever I will be in the future. The words of each poem may differ, but beneath the words is the same whisper: *Dear future me, here is where I am today. This is what I see and notice and care about and wonder.*

Perhaps I feel this way because I grew up in New York City, where every day feels worthy of a postcard. There are an infinite number of cities within this one – depending on the season, the time of day, the weather, the neighbourhood, the mood you're in, how hungry you are, how excited or tired you feel and whether you have somewhere to be or are simply letting the city move you.

You can follow your nose, or your eyes, ears, hands or taste buds. You can let someone else's favourite landmarks lead the way or discover your own secret corners that can't be found on any map.

I loved being a kid in New York City. I love being an adult here too. I hope you'll come visit us someday. In the meantime, I am sending you postcard poems of favourite moments from here.

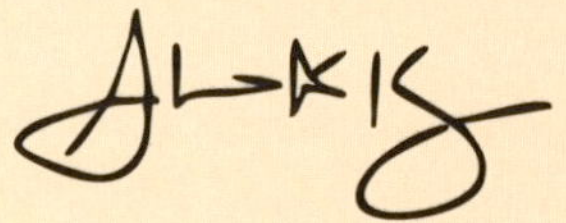

JULY
IV
MDCCLXXVI

City Words

Some days this is a city of nouns:
crosswalk dog poop taxi bus
puddle staircase subway rat
trash tree bicycle building building
tourist neighbour vendor playground

Sometimes the city is all verb:
walking looking
honking barking
working lurking
raining running
riding rushing
meeting seeing
missing kissing
going going

Adjective Day too:
sweaty breezy smelly loud
hungry busy early crowded
late awake and sometimes even
if you can believe it: quiet

TAXI
HONK
TAXI
DELICATESSEN
PIZZ
WOOF!
WOOF!
Hi!
Hi!

We Get Where We Need to Go

by bike or by skateboard,
by taxi, by subway, by bus,
by bridge or by tunnel or by ferry,
in strollers, on shoulders, by wheelchair, on foot.
Escalators, elevators, ramps and stairs.
There are maps and memories to help us,
crosswalks and traffic lights, signs and instructions,
and somebody to ask for directions
if you get turned around.

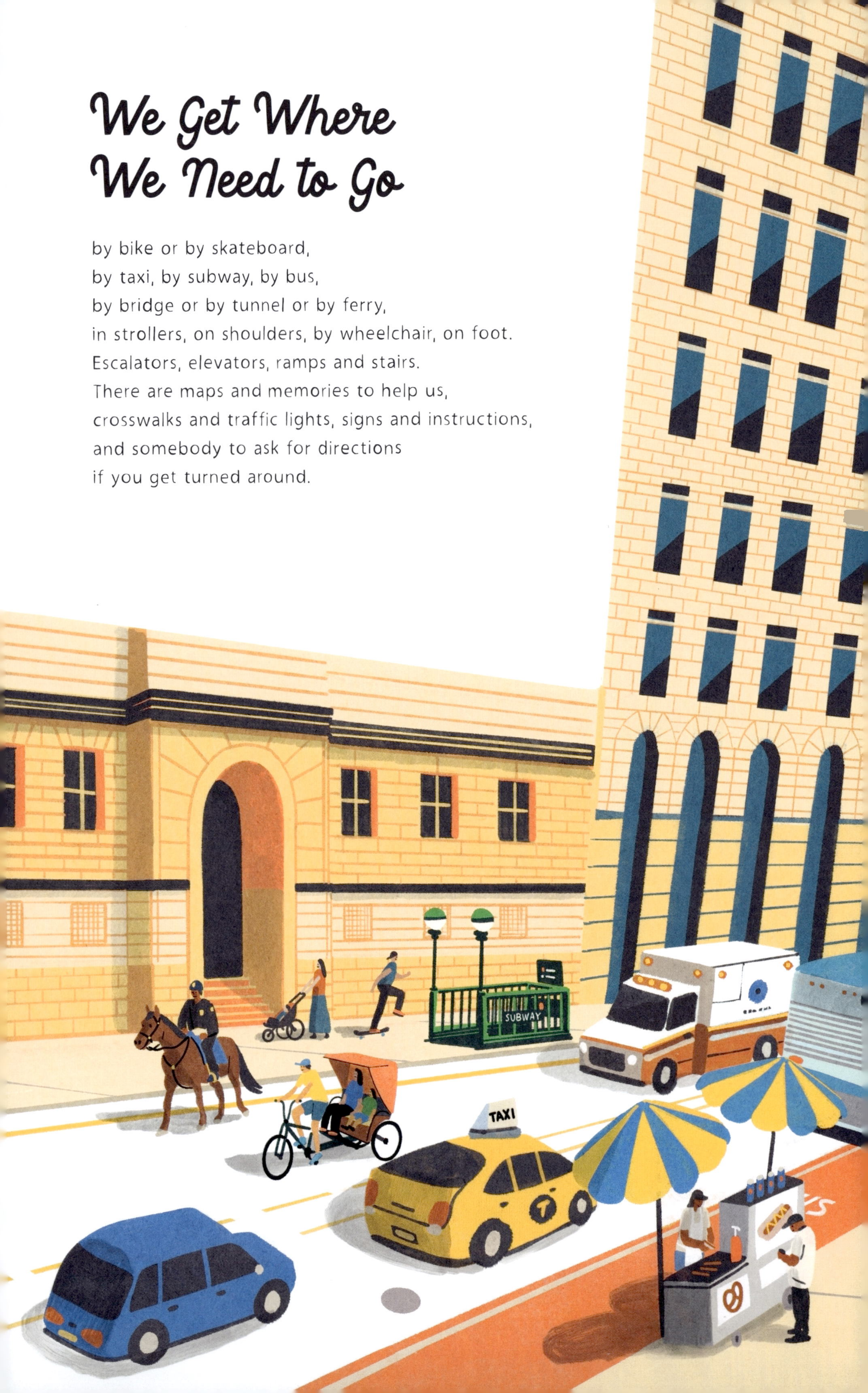

NYC

EAT
LIVE
T·REX
NYC
NEW
CAR

In Times Square

there is something to see in every direction.
Look up: at the billboards, bright lights and marquees.
Look in: at the audiences, the crew, the diners, the waitstaff.
Look out! for the tourists, mascots and commuters,
the buskers and promoters, the artists and vendors.

Hurrying Home

Because I know my neighbourhood so well,
even when I get caught
with no umbrella, I can still
avoid getting drenched on my way home
by zigging and zagging from awning to scaffold.

And my neighbourhood knows me back:
the postman who waves when he drops off the mail,
the cat at the bodega who lets me pet her,
the waitress at my favourite restaurant
who remembers which dish I love.

The Museum of Natural History

The very oldest New Yorkers live at 81st Street and Central Park West.
You might recognise them from books or movies,
but up close they are even more impressive!
They have so much to teach us about a time
before this city (or any city!) was even here.

Like many New Yorkers, their neighbours might
look different – some have gills or beaks or tusks –
but everybody fits, everybody belongs,
everybody has something to share.

Snow Day

There is no better way to spend a blizzard
than slip-sliding through the park.
Nearly anything can be a sled if you want it to be:
a cafeteria tray, the upside-down lid of a garbage can,
when the snow piles up, we all slide down!

Subway Mysteries

What book is he reading?
What is in that bag?
Where are they going?
How can she carry that?
How did they learn how to do that?
How does he get his dog to stay?
Do you think they know each other?
How many more stops are left?

3

Grand Central Secrets

Meet me at the Whispering Walls
in the tunnels of Grand Central Station,
and I will speak softly into the tile,
so the arch can carry my voice above the heads
of the rushing travellers, over the rumble of trains,
and deliver my secret to your ears.

hear me?

The Brooklyn Bridge

means a lot
to a lot of different people.
Maybe it is your favourite place for
a leisurely weekend bike ride,
or part of a daily commute,
where you run in a race,
where you go to take photos,
where you watch the ships and barges go by.

Maybe it is the landmark you look for
that helps you figure out
which direction you are facing;
a reminder that Manhattan
is an island after all.

Blossoms in the Bronx

When you have a few hours to spare,
you can trade in the traffic lights
for trees and flowers, plants and vines,
at the New York Botanical Garden in the Bronx,
a perfect place to lose track of time and do a little wandering,
where the air is sometimes wet,
and bright with petals and sweet to sniff.

A Chorus in Queens

There are more accents and languages spoken in Queens
than anywhere else in the world.
Every city block becomes its own orchestra,
where you can hear sounds you've never heard before,
in harmony with voices that sound like home.

睇多啲書
βιβλία
বই পড়া
читать книги
책을 읽다

Street Scents

How about a bagel with cream cheese and lox?
Or bacon, egg and cheese on a roll,
or dim sum, or roasted nuts, or a hot dog from a cart,
or maybe a pretzel, or maybe kebab,
some apples from the farmer's market,
a soft serve or shaved ice,
a black and white cookie, a slice of pizza?
Sometimes I don't even realise I'm hungry until
the city tells my nose that I am.

AL!
HALAL!
TACO BURRITO

Visiting Coney Island

If you ride the subway to Coney Island,
at the end of the subway is a boardwalk.
And at the end of the boardwalk is a beach,
and next to the beach is The Cyclone –
a roller coaster made of wood and steel
that goes *click clack*, *click clack* the whole way up.

And from the top, for just a moment,
you can spy all the people sunbathing and splashing,
snacking on famous hot dogs and
wandering the famous boardwalk,
before you tip forward and throw up your hands
like others have done before you, for one hundred years!

BOOKS
BUY & SELL
Green Market
52

Popsicle Weather

When the heat becomes unbearable,
relief can be found
in the jingle of the ice cream truck,
the rush of a hydrant,
the kiss of a fountain,
the drip of a popsicle,
a blast of cold air from a shop you don't need anything from,
or didn't until right now.

Seeing Lady Liberty

On the ferry to Staten Island,
you can wave at the Statue of Liberty!
Great copper lady, who has seen
so many boats arrive and depart,
who has seen so many generations of New Yorkers,
and newcomers and visitors,
and now, she has seen you too.

Surprise Celebrations

If a street is cleared of cars, it might be
for a parade or a street fair or a block party,
which are all perfect opportunities for snacks,
and smells, and marching bands, and flags and banners
and the best outfits you've ever seen.

An Evening Stroll

Sometimes I walk through Central Park
with my arms outstretched and say,
Wow! Did you know there is a park here? And so centrally located!
It is a joke for an audience of only fireflies,
who do not laugh, but do, I think,
deserve a performance of their own from time to time,
after all the shows they put on.

There are four-digit numbers on every lamppost in the park,
and if you both know how it works,
you can tell someone where to find you
using only lampposts as your guide.
The city is full of secrets and codes,
never-ending ways to find who or what you are looking for.

6104

The City We Share

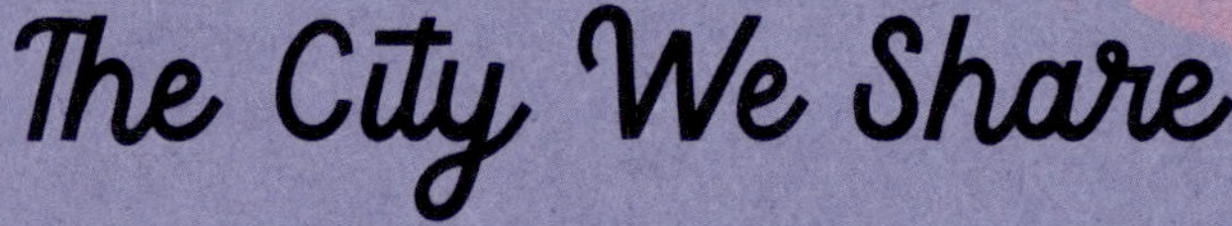

If you leave the city but turn back to look,
you can see its silhouette
like it has been cut out of paper and held up to the light.
From here, it looks like it would fit if you opened your fingers –
all that city in the palm of your hand.

New York Snapshots

New York City is a place where history, art, nature and excitement come together. Whether you're exploring a towering skyscraper, relaxing in a giant park or seeing the sights that make the city famous, there's always something new to discover on the streets of the Big Apple. So, the next time you visit or dream about New York, remember that every corner of the city has a story to tell!

The Statue of Liberty

The Statue of Liberty stands proudly on Liberty Island, greeting visitors from all over the world.

Fun fact: The statue was a gift from France to the United States in 1886, symbolising freedom and friendship.

Did you know? Lady Liberty's full name is *Liberty Enlightening the World*, and she holds a torch that stands 8.8 metres tall!

Central Park

Central Park is located in the middle of Manhattan, perfect for playing, picnicking or just relaxing.

Fun fact: It's larger than 1,700 football fields!

Did you know? Central Park has its own zoo, ice-skating rink, and even a castle called Belvedere Castle.

Coney Island

Coney Island is a fun-filled beachside neighbourhood in Brooklyn, known for its lively boardwalk and thrilling rides.

Fun fact: Coney Island is home to the Cyclone roller coaster, which has been zooming through the air since 1927!

Did you know? It's also the perfect spot to relax on the beach, explore cool museums and enjoy a delicious hot dog at Nathan's Famous!

Brooklyn Bridge

This iconic bridge connects the boroughs of Manhattan and Brooklyn.

Fun fact: When it opened in 1883, it was the longest suspension bridge in the world!

Did you know?
The Brooklyn Bridge was built using steel cables and took 14 years to complete.

Times Square

Times Square is known for its huge, glowing billboards and the hustle and bustle of crowds.

Fun fact: Over 300,000 people pass through Times Square every day!

Did you know? Every New Year's Eve, a giant crystal ball drops from a pole in Times Square to welcome the new year.

At 443 metres, the Empire State Building was the tallest building in the world when it was completed in 1931.

Fun fact: On a clear day, you can see up to 130 kilometres from the top!

Did you know? The Empire State Building gets struck by lightning about 20 times a year! It's made of steel, so it's designed to safely conduct the electricity down to the ground.

Empire State Building